High Powered CVs

If you want to know how...

Planning a Career Change
How to take stock, change course, and secure a better future for yourself

Write a Great CV
Create a powerful CV that really works

CVs for High Flyers
Elevate your career with a CV that gets you noticed

Handling Tough Job Interviews
Be prepared, perform well, get the job

Succeeding at Interviews
Give great answers, ask great questions, get the job you want

howtobooks

Please send for a free copy of the latest catalogue:

How To Books
3 Newtec Place, Magdalen Road,
Oxford OX4 1RE, United Kingdom
email: info@howtobooks.co.uk
http://www.howtobooks.co.uk

High Powered CVs

Powerful application strategies to get you that senior level job

Rachel Bishop-Firth

howtobooks

Published by How To Books Ltd,
3 Newtec Place, Magdalen Road,
Oxford OX4 1RE. United Kingdom.
Tel: (01865) 793806. Fax: (01865) 248780
email: info@howtobooks.co.uk
http://www.howtobooks.co.uk

First edition 2000
Second edition 2002
Third edition 2004

British Library Cataloguing in Publication Data.
A catalogue record for this book is available from the British Library.

Edited by Francesca Mitchell
Cover design by Baseline Arts Ltd, Oxford

Produced for How To Books by Deer Park Productions
Typeset by PDQ Typesetting, Newcastle-under-Lyme, Staffordshire
Printed and bound by Bell & Bain Ltd., Glasgow

NOTE: The material contained in this book is set out in good faith for general
guidance and no liability can be accepted for loss or expense incurred as a
result of relying in particular circumstances on statements made in this book.
Laws and regulations are complex and liable to change, and readers should
check the current position with the relevant authorities before making
personal arrangements.

Contents

Preface

Competition in the job market for senior and professional roles is increasingly fierce, and your CV is a vital tool in winning the post that you want. This book will take you through the process of **preparing a CV that works for you.** It covers:

- deciding on your job search strategy
- identifying your personal key selling points
- grabbing the recruiter's attention to make them read your CV
- choosing an appropriate format and style for your CV
- selling yourself to the employer
- projecting a suitable professional image
- creating a winning covering letter
- using your CV to prepare for your interview.

I would like to dedicate this book to my son David and Elizabeth my daughter. I would also like to thank my husband Andy for keeping David amused while I was writing, and Nick and Sarah Trinder for their help and advice.

With best wishes in your search for a new post,

Rachel Bishop-Firth

Chapter 1

Choosing a Winning Strategy

In this Chapter:

◆ **targeting the right job**

◆ **targeting the right company**

◆ **focusing your search**

◆ **finding the best advertisements**

◆ **accessing the hidden jobs market.**

You can dramatically increase your chances of finding the right post if you plan your jobsearch.

As a manager or professional, your career is important to you. Finding the right role is crucial – and yet you probably have very limited time in which to look for your next post. **Planning your jobsearch strategy is therefore your first step to success.** Decide exactly what kind of work you want, taking into consideration not just the obvious points such as salary and location but also the kind of organisational culture that will enable you to flourish.

Once you know what you want, you can focus your search. Think through how and where you are likely to find the work you want. The hidden jobs market is just as important as job advertisements. Access this hidden market by using your contacts, an agency or headhunter or by making a direct approach to a company that you want to work for.

Is this you?

❓ *I'm just too busy in my current job to look for a new one.*

❓ *I work in a very specialised area, and no one is advertising the kinds of job I want. How am I going to find a new post?*

❓ *I'm applying for dozens of jobs, but getting very few interviews.*

❓ *There are so many good opportunities out there – how do I choose between them all?*

Targeting the right job

Invest some time in defining the role you want. Look at:

◆ responsibilities and type of work

◆ development opportunities

◆ location

◆ salary, benefits and other rewards

◆ organisational culture.

> *Consider whether you could develop your career through temporary or locum posts.*

You may have always looked for permanent roles in the past, but in today's job market many excellent senior jobs are now offered as **fixed term contracts**. Working as a contractor will enable you to:

♦ greatly widen your professional experience

♦ increase your marketability and independence

♦ increase your earnings – often dramatically.

If you are uncertain about what kind of role you want, invest in a session with a **career consultant**. Their services are not cheap, but your career decisions are among the most important that you will ever make. The fees could well be recouped instantly if the consultant helps you win the right job or contract.

Targeting the right company

It is important to consider what kind of **organisational culture** will best suit your working style.

> *Choose to work within companies where you can flourish.*

♦ formal v informal

♦ fast moving v traditional and unchanging

♦ secure v risky and exciting

◆ family friendly v long working hours

◆ European, American or Asian.

Define any other points that are important for you. For example, you may want to work for a company that will pay for your MBA, or you may want exposure to international business, or you may feel strongly about the ethics of the companies that you work for. Your personal circumstances will determine how choosy you can afford to be!

Don't just consider roles in large corporations. **Smaller companies** can offer more excitement and challenge, and give you a role that makes you more marketable when you look for your next post.

Focusing your search

Once you have defined your goals, you can plan how best to achieve them.

> *Make the most effective use of your valuable time by following a well-defined strategy.*

Many job hunters try to maximise their chances of success simply by approaching as many employers as possible with a standard CV and application letter. While this can work, it is usually too haphazard an approach for people at a senior level. Most managers and professionals will achieve greater success if they make fewer approaches to potential employers, but concentrate on getting each of these approaches right.

An effective **strategy** would be to define what kind of work and employer is of most interest – for example, you might want a position marketing electrical equipment for an international company, or to work as a solicitor in a practice in the Bristol area. Then draw up a CV tailored to those opportunities, and send this to the organisations that are most likely to be able to provide you with those roles. Take more time over a few CVs to be sent to those employers that you would most like to work for.

If you are very senior, or there are only a few organisations offering the kind of work that you want, it is worth taking the time to thoroughly research each opportunity and tailor a CV to fit each one.

Finding the best advertisements

Advertisements often offer the quickest and easiest way to find a new job.

> *Find out where the best senior opportunities in your field are advertised both in the traditional media and on the internet.*

Take a look at **internet sites** such as Monster.co.uk, which will send you suitable vacancies as soon as they are registered. Make sure that you are on the subscription lists for the best **journals** in your field. Block out time in your diary on the day that the appointments pages are published in the newspaper or the date that your professional journal arrives, so that you can go through the vacancies advertised. If you wait until you have the time you may never get round to it.

If a post looks interesting, call the company to get some further information about the role and the sort of person they are looking for. This will help you to prepare your CV and covering letter and give you a head start in preparing for your interview.

Accessing the hidden jobs market

A surprising number of vacancies are never advertised. Many managerial and professional posts are filled through:

♦ speculative approaches

♦ agencies

♦ headhunters

♦ contacts.

One way of accessing the hidden jobs market is to **take the initiative** and send out speculative CVs to companies that you know could benefit from your skills and expertise. Look for organisations that are:

♦ expanding their market share or number of clients

◆ being awarded large new orders or contracts

◆ opening new outlets/offices

◆ branching out into your field of expertise

◆ going through a phase in their development where your specialist skills could add value.

To minimise the number of rejections you receive, research using the business/professional press and your contacts is vital.

It is important to make sure that your CV goes to the right person. Once you have found a promising prospect, identify the manager of the department that you want to work for (from the company switchboard if necessary) and give them a call. This is not to try to talk them into giving you a job, but simply to introduce yourself and ask if you can send them your CV.

Send your details to the best recruitment agencies in your field.

A good **agency** will take your CV, find vacancies that would suit you and then market you to the companies offering the opportunities. Agencies often:

◆ have access to the unadvertised jobs market

◆ act as headhunters.

Using an agency is free to the applicant – they make their money through charging the companies that use their services. Only use agencies which have expertise in your field and have a good reputation. Avoid any agency that tries to charge you for finding work, or that tries to insist that you use them exclusively.

The agency will usually want to show your CV to a number of clients. Don't tailor your CV too closely to one particular job or employer when sending an application to an agency.

If you are a mature and experienced manager or professional, your **contacts** may be your best way of finding work. Find ways of enhancing your reputation outside your current firm. Cultivate good relationships with other members of your trade/professional organisation, clients, suppliers and previous employers. Consider speaking at conferences, publishing papers or taking part in the programmes run by your professional organisation. You are more likely to get work from someone who knows and respects you, and may attract the notice of a headhunter.

In summary . . .

- ◆ Make sure that you target the roles that you really want.
- ◆ Make sure that you target organisations where you can really flourish.
- ◆ Focus on the areas which interest you most, and

where you have the best chance of succeeding.

◆ Make good use of job advertisements.

◆ Maximise your chances of success by accessing the hidden jobs market

Chapter 2

Finding Your Key Selling Points

In this Chapter:

◆ **finding out what the employer needs**

◆ **identifying your key selling points**

◆ **dealing constructively with weaknesses.**

Your CV is not your autobiography. It is not even a detailed career history. It is your **personal marketing document** – an advertisement for yourself. You are creating it to persuade the employer that you have what their organisation needs and that they should take the time to meet you and find out more. For this reason, your CV should concentrate on the reasons why the employer would want to take you on. These are your **key selling points**.

You need to be able to show to the recruiter that you have:

◆ the right technical **skills/experience** for their job and organisation

◆ a high level of **interpersonal skills**

◆ the ability to flourish within their company **culture**

◆ at the most senior levels – the ability to **shape** the company culture.

You also need to recognise which points a recruiter might see as weaknesses and deal with these constructively in your CV.

Is this you?

❓ *How do I find out what employers are looking for?*

❓ *I know I've got a lot to offer. What should my CV concentrate on?*

❓ *I'm applying for dozens of jobs but getting very few interviews. How do I improve my CV?*

❓ *It's clear from the advertisement that they are looking for a graduate. I know that I could do the job, but I don't have a degree. How do I handle this?*

Finding out what the employer needs

Something that is a key selling point for one organisation is not necessarily so for another. For example, the fact that you have had international experience might be of great interest to one company but completely irrelevant to another. **Find out what the particular organisation that you are applying to will value.** What are they working to achieve? What kind of people do they need to help them achieve this? You need to understand the company's:

◆ goals

◆ challenges

◆ opportunities

◆ culture

◆ competitors.

> *The first step in creating a successful CV is understanding the needs of the recruiting organisation.*

Advertisements provide direct information on what an individual employer wants and often more subtle clues as well. A company describing itself as 'well established, with prestigious clients' is likely to be very different from one that has placed an advertisement asking for people to work in 'exciting new opportunities'.

Make full use of any other **published information** available to you (including annual reports, the business press and the internet) and also your network of **contacts**. If the advertisement gives the name of someone that you can call for further information, take advantage of this opportunity.

If you do not have time to research each individual company that you apply to, or if the agency handling the application is not revealing the name of their client, make sure that you thoroughly understand the **industry or sectors** that you are applying to work in.

Identifying your key selling points

Once you have identified what the organisation or industry that you are applying to wants from their employees, you can **work out the main reasons why they will want to employ you**. These reasons may include your:

◆ relevant experience

◆ track record of previous successes

◆ relevant qualifications

◆ other personal attributes.

These are the main areas that you will want to advertise to the recruiter, and the basis of your CV.

Ask yourself why this particular organisation should want to recruit you. Then make sure that your CV gives them the answer.

For example, Sue is applying for the post of Facilities Manager at the new Pizza Place head office, which is opening soon. She has identified that for this particular employer, her key selling points will be:

◆ Relevant experience – Sue's eleven years' relevant experience includes opening a new head office.

◆ Track record of previous successes – Pizza Place needs to keep costs low in all areas of their business and Sue is very good at managing budgets and keeping costs down.

♦ Relevant qualifications – Sue is an Associate of the Royal Institution of Chartered Surveyors.

♦ Other personal attributes – the new Pizza Place Facilities Manager will need to manage sizeable teams and Sue has the skills and experience to do this.

Dealing constructively with weaknesses

Identify anything that a recruiter reading your CV could interpret as a weakness, for example a number of breaks in your career history or an unusually high number of previous employers. If this reveals a serious mismatch between the needs of the employer and what you can offer, your application will probably be wasted and you need to consider where you are likely to be more successful.

> *No candidate is perfect. However, you need to recognise what a recruiter might see as your weaker points and decide how to deal with these in your CV.*

If the exercise merely shows that there is a gap between what you can offer and the non-existent perfect candidate, your options are:

♦ **Turn what might be perceived as a weakness to your advantage by showing the recruiter the benefits of your particular set of experiences.**

For example, if you are from a different background to most of an organisation's employees, you can bring in new ideas and a fresh perspective.

◆ **Find strengths that offset your weaknesses.**
For example, if you have held a large number of posts, you have a broad range of experience, and are probably adaptable and full of new ideas. Sell these benefits!

◆ **Write your CV in such a way that the weaker points are either not shown at all, or are not emphasised.**
For example, offset the fact that you do not have a degree by emphasising your abilities, experience and business acumen. Move the 'education and training' section to the end of your CV, so the recruiter only reads this once he or she has seen what you have to offer.

In summary...

◆ **Make sure that you understand the needs of the organisation or industry that you are applying to.**
◆ **Identify the reasons why the employer would want to take you on.**
◆ **Identify what a recruiter might see as your weaknesses. Then decide how you will deal with these.**

Chapter 3

Selling Yourself

In this Chapter:
- **getting your message across**
- **making a powerful first impression**
- **presenting your experience for maximum impact**
- **creating an honest CV.**

A successful CV shows your skills, knowledge and experience in the best possible light. Find the most effective way of getting your message across.

Once you have worked out your key selling points, you know **what** you want to say to the recruiter. However, in order to sell yourself effectively you need to plan **how** you are going to present this information.

Your CV is an advertisement for yourself. Advertisers make sure that they catch the eye of the reader and they make absolutely sure that the reader understands the benefits of buying the product. Taking the same approach with your CV will maximise the impact that it has on the reader.

This does not mean, of course, that your CV should

exaggerate your ability or mislead the recruiter in any way. Your aim should be to **help the recruiter by making sure that they fully understand what you genuinely have to offer their organisation**. You can do this by:

♦ concentrating on the points that will be important to the recruiter

♦ presenting your skills, experience and achievements in a way that does them full justice.

Is this you?

❓ *I have thirty years' experience! How on earth am I going to put this onto one or two pages?*

❓ *I want to make sure that the recruiter takes note of my experience in international markets.*

❓ *My job title is just 'General Manager'. How do I show the employer what an important role this is?*

❓ *I want to make up a fictitious post to hide the fact that I was unemployed for 18 months some years ago. I'm sure a recruiter would never find out.*

Getting your message across

Your first aim is to **make sure that your CV gets read**. Recruiters are busy people. They will usually give each CV a quick scan, pick the best for a more thorough reading, and pick only the very best of those to invite for an interview. Speculative CVs may receive only a cursory glance. It is therefore vital that your CV makes it absolutely clear to the most perfunctory reader what you can offer them.

> *Keep your CV short and to the point.*

This means that **your CV must be short** so that your key selling points really stand out, instead of being buried in a mass of less interesting facts. Aim for:

◆ one A4 page for speculative CVs

◆ two pages for most applications

◆ three pages for applications for very senior jobs.

Concentrate on your key selling points. The aim of a CV is to get an interview, and you only need include information that is going to help you get that interview. The following information can usually be **left out** of a CV:

◆ marital status

◆ numbers and ages of children

◆ any more than an outline of jobs that you did more than 15 years ago

◆ minute details of more recent jobs (you can fill the details in at your interview)

◆ details of your junior schools

- irrelevant, obsolete or lower-level qualifications, e.g. 'O' levels if you have a PhD

- failed examinations

- reasons for leaving jobs

- salary details

- hobbies and interests (if they are TV-watching, Satanism, etc.)

- place of birth

- nationality

- age (many employers like to know your date of birth, but if you prefer you can also leave this out)

- details of your referees

- names of relatives already working for the organisation. This looks unprofessional on a senior CV.

Making a powerful first impression

If your CV starts with a **powerful selling point** that catches the recruiter's eye, he or she is likely to read further to find out all about you. A positive first impression also colours the way that they see the rest of your CV.

> *First impressions count. Make sure that your CV has a strong start.*

The **first and main section** of your CV will almost certainly be 'Career and Achievements', as this is the crucial area that shows that you can do the job on offer. (Possible exceptions to this would be CVs for jobs where qualifications are of paramount importance.) Within **each section** of your CV, put details of your most impressive or relevant achievements at the top of each section.

End your CV on a high note so that you leave the reader with a final positive image of you as he or she puts the CV down. A section on your interesting hobbies or the languages that you speak can be a good way of ending a CV.

Presenting your experience for maximum impact

Make sure that you do yourself justice in the way that you describe yourself in your CV.

◆ give evidence supporting the claims that you make

◆ quantify your achievements

◆ stress your ability to deliver in the most important aspects of your role

◆ use clear and positive language

◆ avoid ambiguity

◆ be professional.

> *Advertisers take a lot of care in preparing the description of their product. You should do the same when describing yourself in your CV.*

Prove to the recruiter that you have what they are looking for by providing **evidence**. It is not enough to say, for example, that you have excellent negotiating or leadership skills. You need to:

◆ give examples of what you have achieved in the past

◆ show where you have overcome difficult challenges in making these achievements

◆ tell the reader how your organisation benefited.

For example, instead of saying: *'I am an excellent leader and build high performance teams'* tell the recruiter *'On taking up the post of European Sales Manager, I set up a team of ten salespeople based in three countries. By focusing on communication, motivation and goal setting, we exceeded demanding sales targets in each of the four years that I held this post.'*

Quantify your achievements to give a more meaningful picture of the size of your role and what you achieved within it. For example:

Staff Nurse Grade D on the Acute Female Surgical Ward (30 beds) or
Managing the accounts of 50 customers

Where possible, you should quantify any improvements

that you have made. For example:

Saved the department £10,000 over 12 months or Increased first-time test passes by 10%

Show your ability to deliver in the most important aspects of your role. This is particularly important if you work in an area where numbers can only ever give a small part of the picture – for example, if you are a caring social worker, a talented designer or an inspiring teacher.

For example, Steve is an Information Technology Project Manager preparing a CV to go to an agency. He can quote some impressive statistics in his CV. He has:

◆ implemented projects with a value of up to £1 million

◆ redeveloped a customer information database holding 20,000 customer records

◆ implemented a payroll system covering 5000 staff.

However, Steve knows that this doesn't tell the whole story. When he writes his CV, he includes the following points:

◆ the projects were completed to clients' time, budget and quality standards

◆ the projects met his clients' ultimate goals – for example, reducing customer complaints or increasing the speed of data access

◆ ongoing support was provided where needed.

Your CV should use **clear and positive language**. Avoid jargon or acronyms unless you are certain they will be understood. Don't pad your writing with phrases like 'duties included' and 'during this time', which add nothing to the information that follows. Use bullet points and start each bullet point with a strong verb. For example, *'During this time I was responsible for family law cases...'* could be rewritten as a bullet point starting: *'Responsible for family law cases...'*. This style avoids the constant repetition of the words 'I' and 'my'.

Avoid ambiguity. Phrases such as *'I supported the change process'* or *'I assisted with financial planning for the company...'* leave the recruiter none the wiser as to what you were actually doing. Maybe you assisted with the financial planning by making the tea and doing the typing for a team of accountants! Make it clear what your contribution was. For example: *'Analysing past financial performance to identify areas for future improvement, preparing budgets and creating financial models to ensure sound financial planning'*.

Recruiters will not take a senior CV seriously unless it is **businesslike and professional**. Don't use jokes or gimmicks.

Creating an honest CV

Your CV should be made up of **positive** information about yourself. You will naturally present your achievements in the best possible light. There will also be information that does not help your case, which you want to leave out. You can usually omit details of failed exams, unsuccessful projects, jobs that lasted just a few weeks, and so on.

> *Your CV must not be economical with the truth. The employer will not recruit you if they discover that you have lied on your CV.*

There is clearly a difference between putting yourself in a positive light and misleading the recruiter.

◆ You may get caught out – many recruiters routinely check applicants' backgrounds.

◆ If you talk yourself into a job that you can't do, you won't last long.

Avoid the temptation to embellish your CV.

In summary . . .

◆ Make sure that your CV is short and to the point, so that you get your message across.

◆ Make a powerful first impression by giving your CV a strong start.

◆ Describe your experience in a way that will make a strong positive impact on the reader.

◆ Create a CV that is both positive and honest.

Chapter 4

Your Career and Achievements

In this Chapter:

- **choosing an appropriate format**
- **the time-based CV**
- **the skills-based CV**
- **summaries.**

A manager's or professional's CV must show a **clear track record of achievement** within their chosen field. Details of your education and outside interests can add weight to your CV, but it is the 'Career and Achievements' section that proves to the recruiter that you have the skills to do (or learn) the job on offer. Your key selling points should come over clearly in this section.

This is the most important part of your CV. Your track record must show the recruiter that you have what it takes to succeed in the post that they are offering.

There are two main ways to present your career and achievements:

- the time-based CV

◆ the skills-based CV.

Each is suitable in different circumstances. Experiment to see which style is best for selling what you have to offer.

Is this you?

❓ *I've got a great portfolio of experience, but I've gained it through working in a large number of jobs.*

❓ *I've only ever worked for one company.*

❓ *How much do I need to say about the jobs that I was doing in the 1960s?*

❓ *How should my CV deal with the fact that I'm currently unemployed?*

❓ *I started right at the bottom and I've worked my way up. My CV needs to show how much I've progressed.*

Choosing an appropriate format

The time-based CV is the traditional style of CV. It gives details of each post that you have held, starting with the most recent and working backwards through time. This is the format preferred by most employers.

> *Sue can show a history of uncomplicated career progression. A time-based CV is therefore the logical choice for her.*

The **skills-based CV** is organised around your skills and knowledge rather than the posts that you have held. Because it emphasises your abilities and your achievements, it is perhaps a more logical way of selling yourself to an employer. Unfortunately, many recruiters suspect that skills-based CVs are used to hide patchy work histories. However, this is a useful format to use where you:

◆ have worked for a large number of employers

◆ have worked in a number of different fields or careers

◆ have had a career break or a number of spells of unemployment

◆ are not currently in work

◆ have developed valuable skills in unpaid work

◆ are applying for a job demanding skills that you possess, but have not used in recent posts

◆ are changing career and want to emphasise your transferable skills.

Steven has spent the last seven years working as a contractor on dozens of short-term projects. The best way that he can summarise this experience for a recruiter is by using a skills-based CV.

SUSAN BROWN
24 Mounds Road, Walton, Hampshire PT29 3QE
Home Telephone: 00000 111 2222
Work Telephone: 11111 222 3333

PROFILE

A professional Facilities Manager with eleven years' experience of managing projects, staff, budgets and contracts to ensure the smooth running of office facilities. Associate of the Royal Institution of Chartered Surveyors.

CAREER AND ACHIEVEMENTS

DATACO HEAD OFFICE, Portsea, Hampshire

Maintenance Manager (June xx – Present)
Managing the maintenance function for a prestigious head office accommodating 300 staff and five regional offices accommodating a total of 500 staff. Achievements include:

◆ Preparing the head office for occupation following Dataco's purchase of the site, including management of a major refurbishment of the ground floor within budget and to a tight deadline.
◆ Preparing and controlling the maintenance budget. Careful control has resulted in costs being below median in every year that benchmarking against similar companies has been undertaken.
◆ Managing all maintenance contracts through the complete process of requirements analysis, tender process, negotiation, development of service level agreements and ongoing management.
◆ Supervising up to 20 maintenance contractors on site.

COLEFAX FACILITIES MANAGEMENT

Project Manager (Feb xx – June xx)
Assistant Project Manager (Sept xx – Feb xx)
Management of increasingly large contracts including the maintenance contracts for DrugStore's Harport Regional Office, and Computerworld's Westport site. Ensuring all maintenance and minor works completed to clients' satisfaction; management of refurbishment projects; developing, agreeing and implementing service level agreements; and developing cost control procedures.

Technical Assistant (June xx – Sept xx)
Training in all aspects of facilities management.

EDUCATION

BSc (Hons) 2:2	Building Surveying, Yorkshire Polytechnic	Sept xx – June xx
3 A levels	North Hill School, London	Sept xx – June xx

ADDITIONAL INFORMATION

◆ Date of Birth xx/xx/xx
◆ Full, clean driving licence
◆ Health – excellent
◆ References available on request
◆ Interests – voluntary work organising outings for disabled children with the Sunshine Trust.

Figure 1. Sue's time-based CV.

Steven Black
2 Heaton Road, Northmoor, South Yorkshire SY34 9LB
Tel/Fax: 00000 11122
Mobile: 1111 666666
E-mail sb@internet.co.uk

PROFILE

An experienced Information Technology Project Manager and Chartered Engineer. Manages the full lifecycle from requirements specification to implementation. Ensures that optimum business solutions are delivered to meet customer requirements within budget.

KEY SKILLS

Project Manager
Implementing projects with a value of up to £1 million to meet clients' time, budget and quality standards. Recent projects have included:

◆ Redeveloping a customer information database to a tight deadline for the Clothesco mail order company. Migrating the records of 20,000 customers from an ICL mainframe to a UNIX (Solaris) platform; improving data quality control methods (e.g. error reporting and change control) to improve accuracy of records and reduce customer complaints. Managing system testing, verification and acceptance of the system.

◆ Analysing the engineering information requirements of North Sea Engineering plc. Designing and implementing a secure company Intranet system to improve the speed of data access, reduce paperwork and ensure that data is up to date. Producing supporting documentation; managing the training of 100 staff at all levels of the organisation in the new system; ensuring a smooth handover to the operational team; and providing ongoing support.

◆ Implementing an Oracle-based payroll system for 5000 staff at Supercorp UK.

Business Systems Analyst
Analysing complex business systems, working closely with clients to ensure a detailed understanding of their needs, and designing a range of solutions. Projects have included:

◆ Analysing and designing a stock control information system for 50 retail outlets in the Cheapprice Shops Group, resulting in a 10% reduction in stock holding costs and faster delivery of merchandise. Finding solutions to conflicting needs of different departments.

◆ Analysing complex business processes and designing business solutions for a wide variety of firms including Pharmco, Supra Cars, Megabank, Tomorrow Group and DrugStore.

Figure 2. Steven's skills-based CV.

INFORMATION TECHNOLOGY

Environments
Intranet, WAN, IBM Mainframe, UNIX (Solaris, HPUX), Novell 4.1, Microsoft Networking, Windows NT, Windows 95, Oracle.

Programming languages
IBM COBOL, C++, dBASE, Turbo Pascal, HTML.

Software
Microsoft Office, Microsoft Project.

Internet
Internet Explorer, Netscape, World Wide Web, HTML, e-mail.

CAREER SUMMARY

Contract Work for a wide variety of blue-chip companies
in the Financial Services, Retail, Mail Order, Manufacturing
and Engineering sectors   June xx – Present

Project Manager	Circo Systems	Feb xx – June xx
Team Leader	Megacomp	Mar xx – Feb xx
Senior Systems Analyst	Megacomp	Nov xx – Mar xx
Computer Programmer/Analyst	World Computer plc	Feb xx – Nov xx
Graduate Trainee	World Computer plc	Sept xx – Feb xx

EDUCATION

BSc (Hons) Electrical & Electronic Engineering 2:1, Southcoast Polytechnic xx – xx
3 'A' levels, 7 'O' levels, Selby Comprehensive, Portchester xx – xx

INTERESTS

I enjoy playing golf and cricket and am currently a member of the Clothesco cricket team.

ADDITIONAL INFORMATION

◆ Full, clean driving licence
◆ Date of birth xx/xx/xx
◆ Health – excellent
◆ References available on request

Figure 2. continued

The time-based CV

Your current or last post will usually be the one of most interest to the recruiter and should therefore be shown first and given the most **space and emphasis**. Less and less detail is needed on each of your previous posts as you work backwards through time, and only a broad outline should be given on roles that you held more than 15 years ago. This keeps your CV to a readable length and focuses the reader's attention on your most recent and relevant achievements.

> *The time-based CV is organised around your career history.*

For each organisation that you have worked for, **you should include:**

◆ The **name of the company** and where they are or were **located**. A short description of the business may help the reader (for example, 'Smith and Jones Ltd are the largest manufacturer of quality widgets in the UK').

◆ **Your job title(s)**, listed in reverse chronological order if you held more than one post with the organisation. If you never had a job title, or your title was confusing or misleading in some way, choose an appropriate name that accurately and honestly reflects what you did. For example, your firm might have called you an 'Operations Support Analyst', but it would be more helpful to tell the recruiter that you were a Market Researcher.

◆ The **dates** that you worked for the company or held each post. If you are still in the job, show this as, for example, 'June 1998 – Present'. For your recent career history, the recruiter will want to know the months that you started and finished in a job as well as the years.

◆ What you **achieved**. This is the core of your CV. Note that the focus should be on achievements rather than just duties. To ensure that the reader focuses on the most important points, you should describe no more than six aspects of your most recent post, and give less detail about previous jobs.

Exercise

◆ Think about each of the last three posts that you have held. What would a recruiter see as your most important achievements during your time in that post?

◆ What are the most important points about this achievement that the recruiter needs to know?

◆ The details of your career and achievements must be clear and easy to read. The best format for **laying out your information** on each post is usually:

Job Title　　　*Name of Company*　　　*Dates post held*
◆ *Achievement*
◆ *Achievement*

What you did in the job will usually be more important

than the company in which you did it, so the job title is placed to the left where it will be the first thing that the reader sees. If the company you worked for was very prestigious, you can reverse these two items. The start and finish dates for each job are of lesser importance, and therefore appear on the right of the page.

If you have **changed career or worked for a wide variety of employers** try to demonstrate that your career has followed a logical pattern. Ideally, you should show how each move developed your skills and abilities further and that there has been an underlying purpose or area of expertise in your career. It could be that your career has been one of caring for children, first as a nurse and then as a teacher; or managing teams, first in the armed forces and then in industry. It also helps if you can show a positive reason for career changes, perhaps because in your first career you were able to identify an area of strength that you wanted to build on.

Never leave unexplained gaps in your career history. A suspicious recruiter may wonder whether you were doing something that you want to hide during that time. If, like an increasing number of job applicants, you were a homemaker, travelling or unemployed for a period, put this information in the correct place in your history. For example:

Job-hunting following redundancy July xx – Sept xx

If you took a few months away from your job due to **maternity leave or long term sickness** but returned to work with the same company, your CV does not have to say that you were not at work during this time.

If you have had **many years of experience with one employer,** it is particularly important to stress that you have grown, progressed and gained a breadth of experience within that organisation. Divide the information that you give on your time with that organisation into a number of subsections. For example:

Senior Research Chemist, Europlastics, Beaconsfield
June xx – Sept xx

◆ xxxxxxxxxxxxxxxxxxxxxxxxxxxxxx
◆ xxxxxxxxxxxxxxxxxxxxxxxxxxxxxxxxxxxxxxxx
◆ xxxxxxxxxxxxxxxxxxxxxxxxxxxxxxxxxxxxxx
◆ xxxxxxxxxxxxxxxxxxxxx

Research Chemist, Europlastics, Dortmund, Germany
August xx – June xx

◆ xxxxxxxxxxxxxxxxxxxxxxxxxxxxxxxxxxxxxxx
◆ xxxxxxxxxxxxxxxxxxxxxxx
◆ xxxxxxxxxxxxxxxxxxxxxxxxxxx

Research Scientist, Mouldings UK (a member of the
Europlastics group), Edinburgh May xx – August xx

◆ xxxxxxxxxxxxxxxxxxxxxxx
◆ xxxxxxxxxxxxxxxxxxxxxxxxxxx

Graduate Trainee, Europlastics, Edinburgh
June xx – May xx

◆ xxxxxxxxxxxxxxxxxxxxxxxxxxx

If you have been **self-employed**, you should identify and

sell your achievements as you would if you had been employed.

The skills-based CV

A skills-based CV enables you to put an emphasis firmly on **what you can do**, rather than when you last did it or when you learnt to do it. For example, Steve's CV shown earlier in this chapter gives information on three skill areas – project management, business systems analysis, and information technology.

> *A skills-based CV is organised around your most relevant and marketable skills.*

Exercise

Look at your key selling points. Think through the last ten years of your career. Then ask yourself:

◆ What are my most marketable skills?

◆ What have I done in the last ten years that proves that I have these skills? What have my most important achievements been?

This can include details of **skills you developed outside regular employment** (in the Territorial Army or voluntary work, for example). However, you need to make sure that the accent is on skills that you developed within your main career.

To maintain a clear focus on your key selling points, your CV should have no more than six skill headings, with no more than six achievements listed under each.

While it is tempting to **copy the section headings** from someone else's CV, this will lead you into difficulties later on as you try and fit your information into unsuitable categories. The skills sections that you choose should reflect your own personal selling points and your unique abilities and career history.

A description of your skills should always be followed by **a summary of your career history**. Ideally, this should be a list of your employers in reverse chronological order, with the posts that you held at each and relevant dates. However, if you have held down a great number of jobs or have had a long career, then this may not be practical. If this is the case, select examples of the companies that you have worked for with an eye to the most recent, most prestigious and those with the closest links to the recruiting company or industry.

Summaries

If you have had a **long career**, your CV should concentrate on posts that you have held in recent years. Much less information needs to be given on earlier jobs, particularly those you held over 15 years ago. Those nearer the end of their working lives might want to show details of whole decades in summary form – for example:

Gained experience of retailing in a number of junior positions – 1960–1970

This prevents valuable space on your CV being taken up with out-of-date information and means that the reader focuses on the information relating to your more recent and relevant career history. Drawing attention away from jobs that you did many years ago is particularly useful if you are over 40 and concerned that you may be discriminated against on the grounds of your age. It is also useful if you have had a change of career or have risen to the top from humble beginnings.

You may need to summarise a period of your career rather than give details of every post that you held during that time.

If you have **changed career**, you will not want to give detailed information on the jobs that you did in your first specialism. You will, however, want to sell the transferable skills that you developed. For example, a businesswoman who originally trained as a nurse might wish to summarise this period as follows:

Registered General Nurse 1976–1987
Gaining full professional qualifications at St Cedric's Hospital, London. Developing my career working in a variety of hospitals, reaching the position of Sister in charge of the Accident and Emergency ward and a team of ten nurses. This experience has given me a high level of

interpersonal skills and the ability to manage a team working under extreme pressure.

If you spent a period of your career working in **short-term jobs**, provide a summary of what you were doing during this time, for example:

Contract Site Manager 1981–1985
Managing teams of builders constructing homes and offices around the UK and Germany. Major employers included:

- *Millar Construction plc*
- *Morgan Homes*
- *A.G. Arthur and Sons*
- *Lloyd and Logan Construction*
- *Jabusch-Wiemer GmbH.*

In summary . . .

- Choose the most appropriate format for your CV.
- Use a time-based CV if you want to emphasise steady progression in your career.
- Use a skills-based CV to focus the recruiter's attention on your skills and experience.
- Where appropriate, use summaries to prevent your CV becoming cluttered with irrelevant detail.

Chapter 5

The Rest of Your CV

In this Chapter:

◆ **the header**

◆ **creating an attention-grabbing profile**

◆ **education, training and memberships**

◆ **hobbies and interests**

◆ **personal details and references**

◆ **your other selling points.**

The 'Career and Achievements' section is the core of your CV and should make up the largest part of the document. Much of the rest of your CV is optional.

Back up your 'Career and Achievements' section with selling points related to your education, training, outside interests and additional skills.

Decide what else will help to sell you to the recruiter. This will probably include:

◆ an eye-catching profile of what you have to offer the recruiter

◆ your education, training and qualifications

◆ details of your involvement with relevant professional bodies

- information on your hobbies and interests, to give a fuller picture of what you are like as a person

- details of additional skills that you can offer – for example, languages or computer languages.

Is this you?

❓ *How much should I say about the degree that I took 20 years ago?*

❓ *Should I list all the courses that my employer has sent me on?*

❓ *I'm worried that I'll be stereotyped as too old to do this job. Do I have to give my date of birth?*

❓ *What personal details do I need to give?*

The header

Head your CV with your name in bold capitals. Use the name by which you are generally known rather than your full legal name. If everyone calls you David Perkins it simply causes confusion if you give your name as Charles David Arthur Perkins. However, avoid nicknames (e.g. 'Dave Perkins') as this looks less professional.

Start your CV in the right way. Make sure that the recruiter is clear what name you like to be known by and how to contact you.

Add your **contact details** under your name. As a minimum, you should give your:

♦ full home address, including postcode

♦ home telephone number, including dialling code (if possible, also include a work number and add a note to let the recruiter know which number is which).

You may also want to add your:

♦ mobile number

♦ fax number

♦ email address.

Only add these extras if they are going to be genuinely useful. Do you check your email daily or just occasionally? If the recruiter calls you on your mobile number, will you be able to speak to him or her – or will you be in a business meeting with your current employer?

If you are based abroad, put your contact details at the end of your CV. This means that the employer reads what you have to offer before they are confronted with the information that arranging an interview with you will take extra effort.

Creating an attention-grabbing profile

A profile is a **summary of your key selling points**, put at the top of the CV to catch the eye of the recruiter.

For example:

Production Manager with ten years' experience in managing the manufacture of electrical and electronic components. Excellent track record of improving quality standards while reducing overheads in unionised environments.

If the profile matches the recruiter's needs, you have given them a good reason to look through the rest of your CV. For this reason, summaries are particularly useful on speculative applications.

A profile at the top of the page showing what you have to offer the recruiter may grab their attention and make them read more.

Some recruiters dislike profiles because so many are just empty hype. When **preparing a profile:**

◆ Keep it factual.

◆ Start with a positive statement of what you are – an 'experienced Optician' or a 'Senior Marine Engineer' for example.

◆ Follow this with a brief statement of your most important key selling points.

◆ Back up each statement you make in the profile with evidence in another part of your CV.

◆ Limit the profile to three sentences.

Education, training and memberships

The summary of your educational background should normally come after the details of your employment.

> *The amount of space you should devote to your education and training depends on the importance that qualifications will have in deciding whether you get the job.*

The most important part of your 'Education and Training' section will be the details of your **professional training**, demonstrating that you have all the necessary qualifications for your role. Either the profile at the top of your CV or your 'Education and Training' section should tell the recruiter that you are a fully qualified professional – for example that you are a State Registered Nurse or Chartered Engineer.

In most cases you should give details of your **school and college education**, listing:

♦ your schools/colleges

♦ the dates you attended them

♦ the qualifications that you gained.

For example:

Business Studies BSc (Hons) 2:2 Bridgethorpe University 1985–1988
3 'A' levels Spelthorpe Technical College 1983–1985

This layout shows the course first, which draws the reader's attention to the qualification that you gained rather than where and when you studied. However, if you want to draw attention to your prestigious university and away from a less relevant degree you would lay this section out as follows:

Oxbridge University *Anthropology BA (Hons) 2:2 1991–1994*

Avoid any ambiguity. For example, stating that you 'studied for your Electrical Engineering BTEC HNC examinations' could mean that you took the course but did not pass the exams.

If you obtained your qualifications abroad, you may need to help the reader to understand the level of these qualifications. For example, a UK employer may not know what a baccalaureate is or what a GPA of 3.8 represents. Provide a few brief words of explanation.

Leave out details of old or irrelevant qualifications. Senior and professional CVs should not include information on any of the following:

◆ dates and grades of 'O' levels, GCSEs, etc.

◆ schools attended before the age of eleven

◆ courses that you failed or were unable to finish

◆ qualifications irrelevant to your present career, for example your secretarial training if you are now a manager.

If you cannot omit the last two without leaving an unexplained gap in your career history, keep the details as brief as possible.

Other information should be given in summary form. If you are a graduate you should not include the full details of your 'A' levels, Highers, HNC, etc. It is usually enough to say that you got 3 'A' levels; the recruiter does not need to know subjects, grades and dates. If you have more than three years' work experience since graduation, the full details of your degree course are no longer relevant. The recruiter will normally only be interested in the title and class of your degree and the date it was awarded. Leave out details of interim grades and your modules taken, unless this has particular relevance to the post you are applying for. For example, if you are applying for a post in Spain, you might want to highlight the fact that your Business degree included courses in Spanish and International Business.

Older candidates may go further and decide that it is irrelevant to put in any details of their secondary schooling. If you have many years of experience but few formal qualifications, then you may decide that a section on your education is irrelevant.

If you have good academic and work-related qualifications but have studied an unrelated subject as a **hobby**, put the details in your 'Hobbies and Interests' section. This avoids distracting the reader's attention from your relevant qualifications.

Don't include copies of your **exam certificates** with your application unless you are specifically asked to.

You should only give details of **work-related short courses** if this information is going to be a selling point because, for example, you have:

◆ been trained in a specific technical skill

◆ earned the necessary licence or safety permit to do a particular job

◆ kept up to date with developments in your field.

In many cases it is better to show that you have developed particular skills through what you have achieved in your job. For example, it is better to give details of negotiations that you have successfully concluded than of the negotiation skills course that you attended.

◆ If you have been given training in a particular area of managerial or interpersonal skills, a recruiter may suspect that this is because you are naturally weak in this area. For example, they may wonder if you have been sent on an assertiveness course because you are too timid.

◆ If you list a large number of courses, you give the impression that you spend a disproportionate amount of time (and company money) on training.

◆ Don't include details of course providers and dates of

your courses unless this adds useful information – for example, showing that the safety certificate that you gained is still valid.

◆ Don't waste space with details of irrelevant courses.

> *Membership of a professional association shows that you are serious about your career.*

Give details of your affiliation to the association(s) that you are a member of and include details of any honorary posts that you have held. If these details come to more than a line or two, organise the information into a section on its own. For example:

Member of the Society of Pipeline Engineers
◆ London Section Chairperson 1997–1998
◆ Member of National Award Committee 1999

Hobbies and interests

It is not always appropriate to add this section to a senior CV. An inexperienced new graduate's hobbies may give valuable information on the individual's leadership potential or ability to work in a team. At a senior level you will be expected to show that you have these qualities through your achievements in your job, with outside interests being used as additional backup only.

> *Information on your hobbies and interests gives the recruiter a fuller idea of what you are like as a person.*

Information on your outside interests may help you in the following ways:

♦ Your interests may give extra evidence that you have particular aptitudes and skills – for example, a flair for organising events or working with people.

♦ Success in outside interests adds weight to the picture you are building of yourself as an achiever.

♦ Outside interests show that you are able to relax and recuperate at the end of a stressful day.

♦ Sporting interests indicate that you are fit and healthy (and might be an asset to the firm's football or cricket team!)

♦ Involvement in the community (for example, in local politics or the Round Table) may indicate that you have a useful network of contacts and/or that you could help generate good local PR for the company.

♦ You may, quite simply, come across as a more interesting person.

If your hobbies and interests add to the evidence that you would succeed in the post on offer, give details of them, but be brief. If your hobbies are watching telly and DIY, don't waste valuable CV space on them.

Be wary of the following:

- Telling the recruiter about very risky or time-consuming hobbies. An employer wants you fit, well and in work and a passion for solo round-the-world sailing trips would interfere with this.

- Admitting to anything that could cause a conflict of interests between you and the employer – for example, running your own part-time business.

- Arousing the prejudices of the reader, particularly in the areas of religion and politics. Don't make statements about your beliefs, unless these are actually relevant to the job on offer. For example, you are unlikely to run into problems if you say 'I am an active member of my local church', but a prospective employer might well be intimidated by an announcement that you are an 'enthusiastic evangelical Christian'.

- Giving an employer a reason to stereotype you, however unfair this may be. It might be best to keep quiet about the fact that you are a train spotter or heavy metal fan.

Details of **voluntary work** (including involvement with the Territorial Army, Police Specials, etc.) should be included in this section. The main exception to this would be where you bridged a gap between jobs with voluntary work, in which case you would show this in the 'Career and Achievements' section of your CV.

Personal details and references

Some of your personal details may, unfortunately, lead

an employer to **stereotype** you. You may be all too aware of the following prejudices:

◆ foreign nationals will have problems with the language and work permits

◆ people with children will not move

◆ only people within a narrow age band will be suitable for the post.

And so on.

When you decide what other personal details to give, you need to be aware of how this information might lead to you being stereotyped. It is your decision whether to include the information.

Many recruiters spend a great deal of time and trouble to select people solely on the basis of their ability to do the job, but unfortunately some do not. **If you think that a particular item may lead to unfair prejudice against you, leave it out**. If you have the misfortune to meet a recruiter who stereotypes people on the basis of (for example) their age, they are much less likely to dismiss your application out of hand once they have interviewed you and found out what you have to offer.

If you are a **foreign national** but have a work permit or do not need a permit to work in this country, make a brief note of this fact. If you have been living in this country for a number of years it can be helpful to state this, as it indicates a familiarity with the culture and language.

You can say that you are in **excellent health** as long your ability to do your job is not impeded by any physical problems. If you cannot honestly say this, then omit this section. If you have a **disability**, you may choose to let the employer know that, for example, you use a wheelchair but you are under no obligation to do so.

If you have a clean, full **driving licence** say so. If you have penalty points on your licence, just say that you have a 'full driving licence'. Do not add the details of any penalty points unless you have specifically been asked to do so.

If you are **willing to relocate**, add a short statement to this effect. Indicate which areas of the world you would be prepared to work in, e.g. 'Prepared to relocate within the UK'. If you are not prepared to relocate, omit this section.

Employers like to know your **date of birth**. Recruiters feel that they can get a better picture of you if they know how old you are. If you omit this information, the recruiter will wonder why and may conclude that it must be because you are 'too old' for the job. Include your date of birth unless you are convinced that doing so will seriously prejudice the employer against your application. Don't give your age, as this will make your CV out of date more quickly. There is also no reason to say where you were born, as this adds no useful information for the employer.

You do *not* need to include details of the following:

◆ **Marital status** (unless you want to capitalise on the common preconceptions that single people are more mobile and married men more dependable). Never say that you are divorced or separated, as these words may arouse unfavourable and unjustified prejudices. If your marriage has broken up, you can say that you are single.

◆ **Children**. Many CVs include the ages, sexes and even the names of the applicant's children. Leave these out. They are irrelevant to your ability to do a job and a prime source of prejudice, particularly if you are female. If you want to emphasise your freedom to relocate or take a job abroad you may want to let the recruiter know that you are child-free.

◆ **Salary** – unless you have specifically been asked to state this. The employer may otherwise decide that your current salary is too high for you to be seriously interested in their job, or too low for you to be senior enough to do it. If you are asked to give details of your salary, include not only your base salary but also brief details of the major benefits that you currently receive (company car, bonus, etc.), as the base salary figure on its own can be very misleading.

As this section has little bearing on your ability to do the job, put your personal details at or near the end of your CV.

> *Don't use up valuable space on your CV with details of your referees.*

The employer doesn't need to know the names and contact details of your referees until the final stages of the selection process. All your CV needs to include is the simple statement 'references available on request'. The exceptions to this rule are where:

◆ your references are from deeply impressive individuals

◆ the employer has asked for details of your references in the advertisement

◆ you are looking for immediate employment or contract work and want to save the recruiter time by giving the names, addresses and telephone numbers of your referees.

Testimonial letters should not be included with senior CVs.

Your other selling points

If there is another point that is a major selling point for you, make it a separate section of your CV. Common additional sections are:

◆ **Languages**. Say whether you are fluent or whether you have a working knowledge (i.e. are reasonably competent, but not fluent). Do not include details of a language unless you have at least a working knowledge of it.

◆ **Computer languages and software packages**. Only include details if the language/package is up to date and you have a good working knowledge of it. If you are an IT specialist, you will need to create separate sections to detail the environments, programming languages, operating systems, software and hardware that you are familiar with. It is often appropriate to do this in your 'Career and Achievements' section.

◆ **Papers, articles or books that you have published** on subjects related to your profession. Put the titles, dates and publishers in a separate section after your educational qualifications. If you have had a large number of works published, list only the most relevant.

◆ **Awards** that you have gained which relate to your profession or studies. If it is not immediately obvious what these are for, include a brief explanation. For example:

Institute of Pipeline Engineers, Gold Medal, 2000
◆ Awarded for best research paper published each year in the field of pipeline engineering research.

In summary . . .

◆ **Make sure the header gives details of what the recruiter should call you and how he or she can get hold of you.**

◆ Consider whether to create an attention-grabbing profile for your CV.

◆ Include relevant details of your education and training and your memberships of professional associations.

◆ Use the section on hobbies and interests to give the recruiter a fuller idea of what you are like as a person.

◆ Decide carefully what other personal details your CV should include and let the recruiter know that you will make references available on request.

◆ If necessary, create additional sections for your other key selling points.

Chapter 6

Making a Professional Approach

In this Chapter:

◆ **creating an eye-catching CV**

◆ **the appropriate use of photographs**

◆ **keeping a copy**

◆ **success with application forms**

◆ **making the most of the internet.**

Your CV or application form should have a highly professional image. A recruiter will typically spend only a couple of minutes scanning each CV. If they cannot see the information that they need right away, or your CV is full of spelling mistakes and badly photocopied on cheap paper, it will go into the reject pile.

Make sure that the appearance of your CV maintains your professional image.

Your CV or application form should:

◆ be clear and easy to read

◆ draw attention to your key selling points

◆ be attractive and professionally presented.

The internet has opened up new ways of sending and displaying CVs. If you are preparing a CV for the internet, you need to take account of how the system works to ensure that your information is easily accessible and appears to best advantage.

Is this you?

❓ *I have been made redundant and money is tight. Do I really need to spend money on getting my CV printed and bound? Photocopies would be cheaper!*

❓ *I work as a designer. Does my CV have to stick to the normal businesslike format or can I be more creative?*

❓ *I know that I'm photogenic. Wouldn't it help if I included a photograph with my CV?*

❓ *How do I go about putting my CV on the internet?*

Creating an eye-catching CV

Your CV should have a clear, attractive and businesslike format.

◆ Your CV should be **no longer than three pages** as an absolute maximum.

◆ Your CV should be **visually attractive,** with the text presented in neat blocks and plenty of blank space on each page. Leave wide margins and clear gaps between each block of text to make the information that you present stand out better.

NAME
Address
Home Telephone: 00000 111 2222
Work Telephone: 11111 222 3333

PROFILE

Xxxxxxxxxxxxxxxxxxxxxxxxxxxxxxxxxxxxxxxxxxxxxxxxxxxxxxxxxxxxxxxxxxxxxxxx
xxxxxxxxxxxxxxxxxxxxxxxxxxxxxxxxxxxxxxxxxxxxxxxxxxxxxxxxxxxxxxxxxxxxxxxxx
xxxxxxxxxxxxxxxxxxxxxxxxxxxxxxx

CAREER AND ACHIEVEMENTS

Job Title	**Company Name / Address**	**Dates**

◆ Xxxxxxxxxxxxxxxxxxxxxxxxxxx
◆ Xxxxxxxxxxxxxxxxxx
◆ Xxxxxxxxxxxxx

Job Title　　　　　　**Company Name / Address**　　　**Dates**
◆ Xxxxxxxxxxxxxxxxxxxxxxxxxxx
◆ Xxxxxxxxxxxxxxxxxx
◆ Xxxxxxxxxxxxx

Job Title　　　　　　**Company Name / Address**　　　**Dates**
◆ Xxxxxxxxxxxxxxxxxxxxxxxxxxx
◆ Xxxxxxxxxxxxxxxxxx
◆ Xxxxxxxxxxxxx

EDUCATION

Qualification　　　　College　　　　　　　　　Dates
Qualification　　　　School　　　　　　　　　Dates

ADDITIONAL INFORMATION

◆ Xxxxxxxxxxx
◆ Xxxxxxxx
◆ Xxxxxxxxxxxxx
◆ Xxxxxxxxxx

Figure 3. Suggested CV layout one.

NAME
Address
Home Telephone: 00000 111 2222
Work Telephone: 11111 222 3333

PROFILE

xxxxxxxxxxxxxxxxxxxxxxxxxxxxxxxxxxxxxxxxxxxxxxxxxxxxxxxxxxxxxxxxxxxxxxxx
xxxxxxxxxxxxxxxxxxxxxxxxxxxxxxxxxxxxxxxxxxxxxxxxxxxxxxxxxxxxxxxxxxxxxxxx
xxxxxxxxxxxxxxxxxxxxxxxxxxxxxxxxxxxxxxxxxxxxxx

KEY SKILLS

First skill
- Xxxxxxxxxxxxxxxxxxxxxxxxxxxxxxxxxxxxxxxxxxxxxxxxxxxxxxxxxxxxxxxxxxxxx
- Xxxxxxxxxxxxxxxxxxxxxxxxxxxxxxxxxxxxxxxxxxxxxxxxxxxxxxxxxxxxxxxxxxx
- Xxxxxxxxxxxxxxxxxxxxxxxxxxxxxxxxxxxxxxxxxxxxxxxxxxxxx

Second skill
- Xxxxxxxxxxxxxxxxxxxxxxxxxxxxxxxxxxxxxxxxxxxxxxxxxxxxxxxxxxxxxxxxxxxxx
- Xxxxxxxxxxxxxxxxxxxxxxxxxxxxxxxxxxxxxxxxxxxxxxxxxxxxxxxxxxxxxxxxxxx
- Xxxxxxxxxxxxxxxxxxxxxxxxxxxxxxxxxxxxxxxxxxxxxxxxxxxxx

Third skill
- Xxxxxxxxxxxxxxxxxxxxxxxxxxxxxxxxxxxxxxxxxxxxxxxxxxxxxxxxxxxxxxxxxxxxx
- Xxxxxxxxxxxxxxxxxxxxxxxxxxxxxxxxxxxxxxxxxxxxxxxxxxxxxxxxxxxxxxxxxxx
- Xxxxxxxxxxxxxxxxxxxxxxxxxxxxxxxxxxxxxxxxxxxxxxxxxxxxx

CAREER SUMMARY

Job Title	Company Name / Address	Dates
Job Title	Company Name / Address	Dates
Job Title	Company Name / Address	Dates

EDUCATION

Qualification	College	Dates
Qualification	School	Dates

ADDITIONAL INFORMATION

- Xxxxxxxxxxxxx
- Xxxxxxxx
- Xxxxxxxxxxx
- Xxxxxxxxxxxxxxx

Figure 4. Suggested CV layout two.

◆ Choose a **consistent style** in which to present your information throughout the CV. For example, you might centralise all the headings and show all dates on the right-hand side of the page. This makes it easier for the reader to find the information that they need in your CV.

Two suggested layouts are shown in Figures 3 and 4.

◆ Choose a **businesslike font** in a reasonable size. Restrict the use of bold and underlined text to the section headings, so that these stand out from the rest of your CV.

◆ Check your **spelling, punctuation and grammar**. If your application is not in your mother tongue, get it checked by a native speaker.

◆ Produce a fresh CV for each application using a **word processor and laser printer**. Manual typewriters and dot matrix printers give an amateurish result. Never send a photocopied CV.

◆ Use a high-quality, heavy A4 **paper** in white or cream, and a good quality envelope.

◆ If you are applying for a very senior job or one in which image is important (for example, sales or PR) you should **bind your CV**, using a high-quality and attractive binder that allows easy removal of the pages for photocopying. Preface your CV with a title page giving your name and contact details, and clip your covering letter to the front of the binder.

If you work in a **creative industry**, you do have more leeway for creativity in your CV than an accountant or solicitor would, but don't let it become gimmicky. A CV is a serious business document and should be presented as such. Your information should be presented as professionally as you would present your design ideas to a client.

A professionally presented CV is expensive, but making the right impression increases your chances of getting the post that you want.

The appropriate use of photographs

You should not normally include a photograph with your CV. People form opinions about you very quickly from your appearance. If you do not fit the recruiter's preconceived image of what the jobholder should look like, your CV will be heading straight for the reject pile.

Occasionally, you will be asked to send in a photograph of yourself. This is usually to assist the employer to remember which candidate is which at the interview stage. But **remember the deep importance of first impressions**. Get your picture taken by a professional photographer. Take great care to dress in a way that will create the right impression, and let the photographer know what image you are aiming to project. Once you have a result that you are happy with, have a stock of pictures printed for future use, as reprints are expensive and take time.

Keeping a copy

Having a copy of each CV and covering letter that you send out will be crucial in helping you to prepare for interviews. Always keep a copy of each, filed with any advertisement or other information about the company that you have, so that you can easily retrieve the details when you need them.

Success with application forms

If a company asks you to complete an application form, **don't send a CV instead** as this may lead to you being automatically rejected.

> *Make sure that your application form concentrates on your key selling points.*

When completing an application form you need to decide how to present your key selling points to maximum advantage within the set format you have been given.

◆ Photocopy the form, do as many rough drafts as necessary and then prepare a perfect final copy.

◆ Don't cram so much information into the space given that it becomes difficult for the reader to pick out the important points. If you really need more space, you can add an extra page or two, but it is best to avoid doing this, as a reader scanning a pile of forms to select those of most interest may fail to read those pages.

◆ The final copy should be free from crossings-out and easy to read – if possible, get it typed.

Making the most of the internet

The internet has opened up new ways for you to sell yourself to an employer.

There are two ways of preparing a CV for the internet:

◆ create your CV as a **site on the World Wide Web**, which recruiters can then access

◆ create a CV as an **email** to send out to recruiters.

Today's software means that **creating a site for your CV on the internet** is quick and easy. In theory, this makes your CV available to tens of thousands of recruiters world-wide. It also opens up all kinds of possibilities for advertising yourself. Your CV can include a 'showcase' of your work – for example, an architect can include photographs of houses he has designed, or a web-page author can give links to sites she has created.

Unfortunately, recruiters rarely have the time to surf the net looking for new employees. You are pretty unlikely to get a call from someone who has stumbled across your page on the web and wants to ask you to an interview. Website CVs are of most use as **backup** to a paper CV containing your web address, or (if you are a consultant) your normal advertising.

If you decide to create a website CV, **concentrate on selling your skills and experience** rather than creating a fancy page. Graphics, video and sound prolong the download time for your page and should only be used where they genuinely add to your message. Check that the finished result is still attractive and legible when viewed through different browsers and when printed out.

It is more likely that you will use the internet to **email your CV to a recruiter**. This enables you to get your CV to a recruiter in minutes rather than days, without having to pay for postage.

♦ **Only email your CV to a company if they have invited you to do so.** Don't send out speculative CVs all over the internet; this kind of junk mail is called 'spamming' and users hate it.

♦ **Put your CV in the main body of the email message.** You can send an attachment as well, but this may not get opened if the recruiter is pushed for time, lacks the right software or is nervous about computer viruses.

♦ **Make sure that the recruiter can read your message.** Unless both you and the recruiter use the same software and the same settings, the document that they receive may look quite different from the one that you saw on your screen. Minimise any problems by writing your CV in plain text, without using formatting such as bold, italics and underlining (you can use capital letters, however). If you are creating your CV as a document to cut and paste into your email message, save it as an ASCII file. Once your CV is complete, email it to yourself to see how it will appear to a recipient and print off a copy to check that it will be legible as a printout. If possible, email it to several friends who use different software to see if they can read it easily. A CV added to the email as an attachment should ideally be created using Microsoft Word, as most recruiters will be able to read a Word document.

♦ Compose the CV so that the **first screen that the reader sees grabs their attention** and makes them scroll down the page to see more. A brief summary of your key selling points is a lot better than your address and telephone number; these can go at the bottom of the page. Enter the vacancy that you are applying for in the 'subject' box of the email and don't include a covering letter.

♦ The internet is not a secure means of sending information. **Never use it to give out information that could be of use to a criminal**, such as your National Insurance number.

In summary . . .

♦ **Make sure that your CV catches the eye of the recruiter for the right reasons – its professional and attractive appearance.**

♦ **Don't send in a photograph unless you are asked to. If** you have to send in a photograph, make sure that it projects the right image.

◆ Keep a copy of your CV for future reference.

◆ If you complete an application form, make sure the content and appearance are professional.

◆ Find out how to use the internet and make use of the opportunities it provides.

Chapter 7

The Covering Letter

In this Chapter:

◆ **introducing yourself to the employer**

◆ **saying what you have to offer**

◆ **setting the scene for the next stage**

◆ **ensuring that your covering letter makes the right impression.**

CVs and application forms should always be sent off with a covering letter.

Your covering letter is the very first thing that the recruiter sees. It is essential that it makes an excellent impression.

This letter should introduce you to the recruiter and persuade them to read your CV. It should be no longer than one page and will usually consist of three paragraphs containing the following information:

◆ why you are writing to the recruiter

◆ how the employer would benefit from taking you on

◆ a closing paragraph stating your wish to meet with the recruiter and an indication of when you could attend an interview.

Like your CV, your covering letter should sell what you have to offer to the recruiter.

Is this you?

❓ *I don't know what to put in my covering letter.*

❓ *Can I suggest a suitable interview date to the recruiter?*

❓ *Does my covering letter have to be produced on a word processor, or can I write it by hand?*

Introducing yourself to the employer

Always send your application to a **named individual**. This is especially important if you are sending in a speculative CV. A manager is more likely to read something that is addressed to them personally. If you are sending in a speculative CV, try to identify which manager to send your letter to through your contacts or even the company switchboard. This should be the manager of the department that you want to work for, rather than the human resources manager.

If possible, contact the manager concerned to find out whether they are likely to have any suitable vacancies in the near future and to ask if you can send in your CV. This again increases your chances that the letter will be read. Make sure that you spell the manager's name right, and only use their first name if you already know them personally.

The first paragraph of your covering letter needs to **let the reader know why you are writing to them**. If you are sending in a CV in response to an advertisement, you need to:

◆ identify exactly which vacancy you are interested in (there may be several)

◆ give the title and date of the publication in which the advertisement appeared

◆ quote any reference number given in the advertisement.

If you are making a speculative application, the first paragraph should say what kind of work you are looking for.

The first paragraph of the covering letter greets the reader and tells them why you are writing.

You need to use this opportunity to get the reader's attention and **sell yourself to them**.

◆ Remind them of any contact you have had in the past (this makes it much more likely they will read on).

◆ Express your interest in working for them.

For example:

Dear Charles,
It was good to meet you last week at the Software

Engineering conference. I was very interested by what you had to say about the possibility of contract work with Megaco...

Dear Miss Smith,
Thank you for taking the time to talk to me yesterday about your vacancy for a Store Manager in your Reading outlet. I have watched DrugStore's recent rapid expansion with great interest...

Your interest must sound genuine, so don't go over the top. Also, remember that your aim is to demonstrate enthusiasm, not to tell the recruiter about how they could further your career. The employer is interested in how *you* could help *them*. **Avoid using the following approaches:**

◆ *I feel that I would be able to gain valuable experience with your company...*

◆ *Having gained several years of experience in business law, I am now keen to develop my career further in a large partnership such as yours...*

◆ *This is an area in which I have always wanted to develop my skills...*

Saying what you have to offer

The second paragraph should draw the recruiter's attention to one or two of **your key selling points** that will be of particular interest to them. Keep this brief. If you try to rewrite everything on your CV the important points will be lost in a mass of detail.

> *It is this information that is going to be of most interest to the recruiter and will make them decide whether or not they are going to read your CV.*

Avoid empty hype. Give concrete information on the skills and experience that you have and perhaps some information on one of your major achievements. Choose something that will get the reader's attention and make them look at your CV to find out more about you. For example:

- ◆ *During my three years as Production Manager with Able Engineering, I reduced product defects by 30%...*

- ◆ *As you can see from my CV, I have worked in retailing for five years...*

- ◆ *I am a seasoned Petroleum Engineer, with experience of working in North Africa and the Middle East...*

Avoid lecturing the employer on how to run their business and never say straight out that you understand that they have a problem. Managers will not enjoy being told outright that (for example) their organisation is overstaffed and customer complaints are going through the roof. Keep your statements neutral, for example:

- ◆ *While at Zedco Limited, I reduced staff costs by 25%...*

- ◆ *I have extensive experience in improving customer service in a competitive marketplace...*

Make sure that all the claims you make are backed up with evidence in your CV.

Setting the scene for the next stage

Don't let your letter tail off with a lame 'yours sincerely'.

Close with a strong positive paragraph setting the scene for the next stage – the recruiter asking you to attend an interview. For example:

- *I would welcome the opportunity to discuss this with you further. I will be on leave in the UK between 1ˢᵗ and 14ᵗʰ June and could attend an interview at any time during this fortnight.*

- *I look forward to meeting you and could attend an interview at short notice.*

Always leave it up to the recruiter to decide if they would like to see you. You could, however, follow up the speculative CV with a call to check that the employer has received your CV and ask politely if they would like to see you.

Finish the letter with 'Yours sincerely' if you are writing to a named individual. If you have written to 'Dear Sir/ Madam', then the ending is 'Yours faithfully'. Beneath this should come your signature (preferably in ink, which conveys a more professional image than biro) and then your name typed or printed in full.

Ensuring that your covering letter makes the right impression

Make sure that the appearance of your letter is suitably professional. The covering letter for a senior CV should be produced on a word processor, using the same paper and typeface as the CV. Make sure that it is well laid-out, clear and easy to read. The paper should be white or cream.

An example of a covering letter

Sue is sending a speculative CV to Pizza Place in her search for a position as a Facilities Manager.

This letter has a good chance of success:

25th July xxxx   24 Mounds Road
                                                  Walton
                                                  Hampshire
                                                  PT29 3QE

Dear Alan Green,

Re: Facilities Management Post

Thank you for taking the time to talk to me this morning.

I was very interested to hear that Pizza Place will be opening their new head office in Shorely early next year and that you will be recruiting a Facilities Manager for the site. I successfully prepared the Dataco head office for occupation within budget

---

and to a tight deadline. I have also managed all aspects of maintenance for six Dataco offices, accommodating 800 staff. Setting up and running the Facilities Management department at your new head office would be a challenge that I would relish.

I have enclosed my CV, which I hope you will find of interest. The opportunity to discuss this post further with you would be very welcome.

Yours sincerely,

Susan Brown (Mrs)

Figure 5. Sue's covering letter.

♦ Sue has found out which company is going to occupy a new office complex being built in her area, identified the Property Manager within that company and spoken to him to ascertain that he will need a Facilities Manager. Her CV is going to the right person and there is a very good chance that it will be read.

♦ Sue has set the right tone by thanking Alan Green for taking the time to speak to her. The reader is tactfully reminded of what their discussion was about which will be useful when Alan receives the letter several days later.

♦ Sue shows that she can offer the skills that Pizza Place needs in getting the new head office up and running and expresses enthusiasm for the job.

◆ The letter finishes in a positive manner, and points the way for Alan Green to invite her for interview.

In summary . . .

◆ Introduce yourself to the recruiter and make sure it is clear why you are writing in.
◆ Let them know what you have to offer.
◆ Give your letter a strong positive finish.
◆ Ensure that your letter makes the right impression.

Chapter 8

Taking the Next Step

In this Chapter:

♦ **preparing for the recruiter's response**

♦ **preparing for your interview**

♦ **preparing for a job offer**

♦ **revisiting your CV.**

Use your CV to help you prepare for the next step in your job search – meeting the recruiter.

As soon as you have sent your CV to the recruiter, you need to start preparing for their response. Your CV has created a professional image, and this must be backed up by the impression that you give when the recruiter contacts you. You also need to start preparing for your interview, as you may be asked to attend at short notice, and even for a possible job offer – the employer may need to check your qualifications and references quickly if they decide to offer you the job.

Is this you?

❓ *I have three children at home, and they may well answer the phone to a recruiter calling to talk to me.*

❓ *How can I make sure that the interview goes my way?*

❓ *Things didn't work out for me in my last job. What do I do about a reference?*

Preparing for the recruiter's response

After the care that you have taken to project a professional image in your CV, don't let yourself down by the impression given when the recruiter phones you at home, or by a slow response to their emails and correspondence.

◆ Make sure that your **answerphone** message is appropriately businesslike, and check for messages daily.

◆ Make sure that everyone in your household understands the important of taking down **phone messages** accurately and then passing them on.

◆ If you have given out your **fax number or email address**, check your inbox every day.

Preparing for your interview

Build on the work which you have put into creating your CV to make sure that you give a great interview:

◆ research the organisation/sector

◆ practise selling your strongest points

◆ decide how you will tackle questions about your weaker areas.

At a senior level you will have to demonstrate at your interview a real understanding of the **organisation and sector** in which you are applying to work. Make sure that you can talk knowledgeably about developments in your specialist field and also the organisation's:

◆ financial position

◆ products and services

◆ culture

◆ likely future direction

◆ strengths, weaknesses, opportunities and threats

◆ market position and competitors.

Think through how you can most effectively sell your strongest points.

> *The interview is your chance to expand on your achievements in the detail that you had to leave out of the CV.*

Decide:

◆ how you are going to ensure that each point is covered in the discussion

◆ what you want to tell the interviewer about each point.

Remember that the interviewer will often want to probe

not just what you have achieved but how you achieved it. For example, if your CV shows that you doubled sales within your area within three years, the interviewer will want to know how you went about this. Did you reach these figures through developing positive and sustainable relationships with customers – or through aggressive hard sell to people who will never order again? Did you manage to maintain harmonious relations with the production department throughout – or did you land them with orders that they couldn't fill?

Revisit your strong points just before the interview. This will remind you of the points that you want to talk about in the interview – and looking at all your past achievements will be a great confidence booster.

You will also need to take a look at the weak points in your CV which an interviewer will want to probe.

It is a lot harder to hide weaknesses in an interview than it is in a CV.

Think through how you will answer questions in these areas to show that:

◆ an apparent weakness could be turned to an advantage, and/or

◆ you have compensating strengths, and/or

◆ you will overcome the weakness, and/or

◆ you will minimise the effect that the weakness has on the firm.

For example, if you are applying for an overseas assignment but you have never worked abroad before, you could tell the interviewer about the year you spent studying abroad as part of your degree course and the many short business trips abroad that you have made.

You might decide to **tackle the issue yourself** before the interviewer asks any questions. This is a valuable tactic where you know that an employer may make unfounded assumptions about you (for example, if you are concerned that they may incorrectly be assuming that your family circumstances would make it difficult for you to relocate).

Finally, print **two copies of your CV** to take to the interview. One is for you, and the other for the interviewer – just in case their copy has gone astray.

Preparing for a job offer

Prepare as soon as possible for a job offer. The recruiter is likely to make an initial exploration of your **salary aspirations** during your interview, and you may even get an on-the-spot job offer. To prevent any delays, it is also worthwhile:

◆ ensuring that you have lined up all the background **documentation** that a recruiter may ask for if they offer you a job

◆ establishing your source of **references**.

---

*Many recruiters will not finalise a job offer until they
have seen proof of your qualifications and checked out
your references.*

Set your targets for pay negotiations. Work out your
current total salary package, taking into account all the
benefits that you receive, including bonus, car or car
allowance, shares offers, perks, holidays etc. Try to set a
cash value for each so that you can fairly weigh up what
the recruiter is offering you. What is the minimum that
you are prepared to accept, and what is your realistic
target? How are you going to persuade the recruiter that
you are worth the target amount?

Make sure that you have to hand copies of all the
documents that you will need to send to the recruiter if
you are offered the job. Information that you are likely
to have to show the employer includes:

◆ Copies of your **qualification certificates.**

◆ Proof that you have the **right to live and work in this
country** (note: current UK Home Office guidelines
mean that some companies ask all new recruits to
prove they have the right to work in Britain.

◆ If you are looking for work abroad or applying for a
post in an industry where security is crucial, your
birth certificate and an **up-to-date passport**.

- Proofs that you have completed any **safety training** mandatory in your industry.

You will need to be able to provide the recruiter with **references** from at least two people.

Decide now who you will ask to give you a reference, and whether this might give rise to any problems that you could defuse now.

References for senior posts should always be from people who have known you at work and should include your last manager. Wherever possible, check beforehand that the person you have named is happy to provide you with a reference – although for obvious reasons it will not be possible to do this where the referee is your current manager. Recruiters will only contact your referees when they have made or are on the point of making you a firm job offer, and will let you know before they do so. This gives you a chance to give some advance warning to your referee. Give your referees a copy of your CV to assist them when the time comes for them to provide the reference.

If you are going to have **problems with getting a good reference** from a previous employer, make provision for this now. Even if you did not leave your last employer on good terms, speak to them now to see if they would be prepared to give you an acceptable reference.

> *Firms are usually unwilling to give a bad reference and most will be prepared to at least give a new employer a carefully noncommittal account of you.*

If you are in the process of negotiating your departure from the firm, provision of a reference is an essential point in the discussions. If an employer **refuses to give you an acceptable reference**, you will need to prepare a good explanation for the recruiter of why you have a problem with that employer and be able to offer two very good alternative references.

Revisiting your CV

As you make applications and go to interviews, you will get a better idea of what works in your CV and what can be improved. Some recruiters may even give you direct feedback. Use this information to **improve your CV** and therefore your chances of getting the post that you want.

Once you are in your new job, **carry on improving your CV.** Developing your career is an ongoing process. Think about whether there is anything that you could do now that would be a real addition to your CV the next time you are looking for work. Is there any strong point that you could develop further? If there a weakness that you should work on? Do you need to build up a better network of contacts? **Update your CV every six months** and keep a stock of current CVs on hand.

> *The next time that you find out about a promising new career opportunity, you'll be ready to meet it.*

In summary . . .

- ◆ Make sure that you are ready to respond promptly and professionally to approaches from recruiters.
- ◆ Get ready to give great interviews.
- ◆ Be prepared to discuss your salary aspirations in your interview – and have your references and background paperwork lined up.
- ◆ Keep developing your CV now and in the future.

Good luck with your application!

Appendix– Sample CVs

Brian White

Brian is looking for a new post as a Human Resources Manager. He has created a time-based CV (Figure 6) which he is sending out to agencies. This CV covers the full spectrum of the work that Brian has been involved in: compensation and benefits, industrial relations, training, recruitment and personnel administration.

He has also created a skills-based CV in response to an advertisement for a Training Manager's role (Figure 7). The skills-based style he has used enables him to focus the CV on his experience in training and development.

BRIAN WHITE
87 Chambers Walk, Crawton, Surrey, GT7 9XQ
Telephone: 01234-567890 (Home) 01234-876543 (Office)

Profile

A Human Resources Manager with a wide range of experience in the engineering industry. An expert in providing the full range of Personnel and Training services, including compensation and benefits, industrial relations and payroll management.

Careers and Achievements to Date

British Engineering (Aeronautical Division) Crawton, Surrey
The Aeronautical Division of BE employs a 400-strong workforce in the design and manufacture of sophisticated electrical systems used in civilian aircraft. The division is based on a greenfield site and annual turnover is £100 million.

Human Resources Manager (March XX – Present)
◆ Reporting to the Director and General Manager, managing a team of up to five staff to provide a full Human Resources support service to the Aeronautical Division.
◆ Devising and implementing HR strategies to support the Division in meeting its business aims of quality improvement and cost reduction. Providing compensation and benefits, industrial relations, training, recruitment, database and payroll management and personnel administration services.
◆ Successfully managing the downsizing of the workforce from 600 to 400 staff in a unionised environment without industrial action or disruption to production. Handling redundancies, redeployment and TUPE transfers of staff.
◆ Negotiating the introduction of a new broad-band reward scheme to link pay with individual performance and the salary market.

Training Manager (Feb XX – Feb XX)
◆ Liaising with the management team to analyse development needs for the Division, and implement effective training solutions.
◆ Meeting the division's need to improve the technical skills of manufacturing staff with the introduction of training to NVQ standards. This has contributed to a 12% fall in the number of units rejected during quality inspection.

British Engineering Motor Components Ltd Petersham, Cambs (July XX – Feb XX)
BEMC employs 3,000 staff based over four sites in the south and Midlands.

Personnel Manager
◆ Reporting to the Personnel Director, managing a team of three staff to provide a full Personnel and Administration support service to the Petersham site.
◆ Managing industrial relations, moving from a traditional unionised manufacturing culture towards more effective working relationships.

Figure 6. Brian's time-based CV.

Previous experience

I built up experience in a variety of Personnel and Training roles within a number of British Engineering companies between September XXXX and February XXXX. This experience included:

♦ Designing and delivering management, interpersonal skills, and induction courses to staff at all levels.
♦ Providing a generalist Personnel service.

Between February XXXX and September XXXX I built up experience in a variety of clerical jobs in Coshall, Cheshire.

Interests

I am a keen runner and cyclist. I enjoy taking part in fun runs and charity cycle rides.

Additional Information

♦ Willing to relocate within the UK and travel worldwide
♦ Clean, full driving licence
♦ Health – excellent
♦ References available on request

BRIAN WHITE
87 Chambers Walk, Crawton, Surrey, GT7 9XQ
Telephone: 01234-567890 (Home) 01234-876543 (Office)

Profile

An experienced Training Manager with a wide range of experience in the engineering industry. An expert in providing training and development solutions to meet business needs.

Key Skills

Training and Development

◆ Providing a full Training and Development support service to the British Engineering Aeronautical Division (BEAeD), an operation employing 600 people in the manufacture of sophisticated electronic control systems. Working with the management team to analyse the company's training and development needs and implement effective solutions.
◆ Purchasing IT; management and interpersonal skills; health and safety; and technical skills training courses. Achieving a 30% saving in the BEAeD Training and Development budget through effective targeting of training courses and outsourcing IT skills training through competitive tender.
◆ Initiating the successful launch of an Open Learning Centre at BEAeD.
◆ Designing and delivering management, interpersonal skills, and induction courses to staff at all levels within a number of British Engineering divisions.

Management Development

◆ Introducing a Personal Development Programme for managers and selected high-potential British Engineering employees in association with Oak Hall Consultants. 70% of participants' managers rated this programme 'excellent' or 'very good' at improving the skills of their people.
◆ Managing the BEAeD succession planning, management development and graduate training programmes to ensure that key roles are filled by highly competent and motivated employees.

Technical Skills Training

◆ Meeting the BEAeD's need to improve the technical skills of manufacturing staff with the introduction of training to NVQ standards. This has contributed to a 12% fall in the number of units rejected during quality inspection.
◆ Setting up and supervising apprenticeship and modern apprenticeship training schemes.

Generalist HR Management

◆ Devising and implementing HR strategies to support the BEAeD in meeting its business aims of quality improvement and cost reduction. Providing compensation and benefits, industrial relations, recruitment, database and payroll management and personnel administration services.
◆ Managing industrial relations, moving from a traditional unionised manufacturing culture towards more effective working relationships.

Figure 7. Brian's skills-based CV.

Career Summary

British Engineering (Aeronautical Division) Crawton, Surrey

◆ Human Resources Manager (March XX – Present)
◆ Training Manager (Feb XX – Feb XX)

British Engineering Motor Components Ltd Petersham, Cambs

◆ Personnel Manager (July XX – Feb XX)

Motor Components, Light Engineering and Heavy Engineering divisions of British Engineering (Sept XX – Feb XX)

◆ A variety of Training and Personnel roles.

Between February XXXX and September XXXX I built up experience in a variety of clerical jobs in Coshall, Cheshire.

Interests

I am a keen runner and cyclist. I enjoy taking part in fun runs and charity cycle rides.

Additional Information

◆ Willing to relocate with in the UK and travel worldwide
◆ Clean, full driving licence
◆ Health – excellent
◆ References available on request

Sharon Jones

Sharon Jones is an English teacher and Assistant Head of her department. She has created a CV (Figure 8) to send out in response to an advertisement placed in a national newspaper by a high-performing comprehensive school for a Head of English. She has highlighted the following information:

She has very relevant experience as Assistant Head of Department in a high-performing comprehensive school, and she is ambitious to go further.

She has been part of a team which has raised the standards of English teaching within her school.

She has regularly gone above and beyond what could be seen as the normal boundaries of her job for example, by running the school drama club, setting up study skills courses and supporting other school productions and activities.

SHARON JONES
12 Ellesmere Gardens, Heaton, Lancashire MW12 345
Home Telephone: 0000 – 1111 – 2222
Email: s_green500@maillink.com

PROFILE

A dedicated and experienced Assistant Head of English, who enjoys building a team to provide the best possible teaching to all pupils and who is ready to make the step up to Head of Department.

CAREER AND ACHIEVEMENTS

Assistant Head of English	**Park Road Comprehensive School, Heaton, Lancashire**	**Sept XX – Present**

Park Road Comprehensive School is a mixed-sex, urban school rated as 'excellent' by OFSTED. There are 900 pupils, with 150 in the sixth form.

◆ With the Head of English, managing a team of 4 teachers to provide stimulating and appropriate teaching of English Language and Literature to pupils with a wide range of abilities. The team's achievements include:
  – Raising the school's English Language and Literature GCSE grade A–C pass rates from 40% to 60% within 4 years through managing the introduction of regular testing and mock examinations, providing remedial help where needed, choosing a syllabus which pupils find interesting and relevant and providing training in study skills.
  – Raising the number of pupils choosing to take A-level English by 25% within 4 years.
◆ Delivering the National Curriculum to pupils at Key Stages 3 and 4. Preparing students for GCSE and A-level examinations.
◆ Running the school drama club, which regularly produces popular plays including 'The Crucible' and 'A Midsummer Night's Dream'.
◆ Setting up and running study skills courses for students at GCSE and A-level.

Teacher of English	**Park Road Comprehensive School**	**Sept XX – July XX**

◆ Teaching English Language and Literature to pupils at all levels of ability.
◆ Organising school trips of up to 50 pupils to see plays in local theatres.
◆ Working as one of a team of 3 teachers running the drama club.

Exchange Teacher	**Woolalong School, Australia**	**Sept XX – July XX**

◆ Expanding my horizons as one of a few teachers selected to take part in an exchange programme with Australian schools.

Teacher of English	**Park Road Comprehensive School**	**Sept XX – July XX**

◆ Please see above

Teaching Experience	**Town Road Secondary School London**	**XXXX**

◆ Teaching English to a challenging group of pupils in an inner-city school as part of my PGCE course.

Figure 8. Sharon's CV.

EDUCATION

Postgraduate Certificate of Education (Pass)	Liverpool College	XXXX–XXXX
English BA (Hons) Class 2:1	Midfield University	XXXX–XXXX
A-level English (B), Drama (B) and French (B)	St Swithin's School Lancaster	XXXX–XXXX

ADDITIONAL INFORMATION

- Date of birth XX/XX/XX
- Full clean driving licence; experienced minibus driver
- Excellent health
- References available on request
- My main hobby is music. I play the piano (grade 5) and flute (grade 4), often in support of school productions and activities. I also enjoy singing and am a very active member of a church choir.

Tom Evans

Tom Evans is a Graphical Designer who is looking for a new role through a number of agencies. He therefore needs a CV which covers the full spectrum of the work that he has undertaken. He has worked in varied roles for eight main employers as well as simultaneously undertaking freelance commissions. Because of this, a traditional time-based CV would be hard to follow. Tom has therefore created a skills-based CV (Figure 9) which allows him to group together the different kinds of work that he has undertaken: marketing materials, packaging design, corporate branding and communications, Internet and Intranet design and management of teams.

TOM EVANS
Flat 12, 37 West Street, London NE1 2AB
Home Telephone: 0000 – 111 — 2222
Work Telephone: 1111 – 222 – 3333

PROFILE

A versatile and creative Graphic Designer who has made a major contribution to nation-wide promotional campaigns. Skilled in the design of marketing, advertising, packaging and corporate communication materials including internet and intranet WebPages. An effective team manager, able to manage projects from concept to production and to meet tight deadlines.

KEY SKILLS

Design of Marketing Materials

- Design of marketing materials from concept through to delivery of the finished product, including posters, brochures, flyers, magazine advertisements and point of sale materials, supporting major nation-wide advertising campaigns.
- Experienced in working solo and as part of an agency or client team.
- Illustration and copywriting for all types of marketing materials.
- Experienced in producing materials for both retail and business-to-business advertising.
- Clients include Fizzco drinks (Topical Sun campaign – runner up in the Food Advertising Industry Awards), Sabre Cars (Z model launch) and Datacom Computers.

Packaging Design

- Design of product packaging for a wide variety of retail and business-to-business goods, including luxury, child-oriented, fast-moving and perishable goods.
- Clients include: The Old-Fashion Sweet Company (range of chocolate confectionery), KidKo Toys (Holly Dolls, Plastibricks), The American Coffee Co. (disposable cups, napkins) and Timeco (packaging for watches).

Corporate Branding and Communications

- Design of corporate logos, letterheads, business cards and business gifts consistent with company style and identity for business including British Utilities and KidKo.
- Managing corporate rebranding exercises for Sunshine Holidays and the Disabled Children's Foundation to ensure effective communication of the organisation's image to customers, employees and clients.
- Designing and producing in-house journals and other in-house communication materials for major companies including British Utilities (30,000 employees) and Sabre Cars (15,000 employees).

Figure 9. Tom's skills-based CV.

Internet and Intranet Design

◆ Managing the design of/personally designing websites, including the management of information technology specialists working on design teams.
◆ Delivering internet sites attracting up to 10,000 hits per day to clients including The Consumer Bureau and the Heart Research Foundation. (Sites can be viewed at www.complaints.co and www.hrf.co)
◆ Producing Intranets to communicate corporate messages to the employees of companies with up to 30,000 staff, including Insureco, British Utilities and Wham Records.

Management

◆ Managing teams of up to 8 design staff, working on multiple projects and to tight deadlines in both agency and in-house situations.
◆ Managing the subcontracting of work to photographers, illustrators, copywriters and printers to ensure high standards achieved and target delivery dates met.

CAREER SUMMARY

Associate Design Director	Imageworks	Feb XX – Present
Corporate Communications Manager	British Utilities	March XX – Feb XX
Design Manager	Sabre Cars	May XX – March XX
Design Consultant	Adco	Dec XX – May XX
Senior Designer	Adco	May XX – Dec XX
Full-time Freelancer	New Look	Nov XX – May XX
Senior Designer	The Image Shop	July XX – Nov XX
Designer	Graphco	Sept XX – July XX

Between XXXX and XXXX I also undertook numerous freelance commissions.

EDUCATION

BTEC HND in Graphic Design	Fens College	XXXX – XXXX
BTEC HNC in Graphic Design	Fens College	XXXX – XXXX
A-level Art, 6 O-levels	Amborne College	XXXX – XXXX

ADDITIONAL INFORMATION

◆ Skilled in a wide variety of design packages and Internet authoring software, including Photoworks, Drawsoft and Webgraph.
◆ Date of birth XX/XX/XX
◆ Willing to work anywhere within Europe and North America
◆ Excellent references available on request

Alison Smith

Alison Smith has worked for Bowes China for 20 years, enjoying steady progression up to her current role as Production Manager. A contact has told her that the Production Manager in another local ceramics firm has resigned. This firm is larger and offers better opportunities than Alison's current employer. She has decided to get her CV to the Director of Production within this firm before the job is advertised more generally.

Alison's time-based CV (Figure 10) enables her to emphasise that while she has had only one employer, she has progressed and grown during the course of her career.

Alison Smith
56, Long Street, Northtown, Staffordshire SR5 6CD
Home Telephone: 11111 – 999 – 8888
Work Telephone: 88888 – 999 – 0000

PROFILE

A Production Manager with twenty years' experience in the ceramics industry and an excellent track record of introducing improvements. Chartered Engineer and MBA graduate.

CAREER AND ACHIEVEMENTS

Production Manager   **Bowes China Ltd**   Dec XX – Present
                           Northtown, Staffs

◆ Reporting to the Director and General Manager, managing the production of 400 domestic china products on 5 production lines during a time of expansion for the company.
◆ Leading a production team of 100, working a 2-shift system. Over three years, reducing absenteeism by 25% and staff turnover by 20% by setting targets, improving recruitment and training methods, improving communication with the workforce and effectively handling individual problem cases.
◆ Saving the company £100,000 per annum through reducing the number of products failed at quality inspection, by introducing quality circles and making technical changes and management changes identified by these circles.
◆ Introducing Quality Standard ISO 9001 to the Production Department and ensuring full compliance with this standard, which has helped Bowes China win new orders from clients.
◆ Managing the installation of new equipment worth £3 million to a tight schedule to ensure that new orders could be met.

Production Supervisor   **Bowes China Ltd**   Mar XX – Dec XX
                           Northtown, Staffs

◆ Reporting to the Production Manager, managing 2 production lines and a team of 40 staff.
◆ Designing and introducing a production information reporting system used throughout the department to monitor production quantities, quality standards and safety statistics.
◆ Reducing time lost through accidents in the team by 30% through active leadership and communication on safety issues.

Figure 10. Alison's time-based CV.

Research Technician	Bowes China Ltd Northtown, Staffs	Sept XX – Feb XX

- Undertaking technical investigations into the causes of production faults and proposing solutions to the Production Manager.
- Assisting line managers to make modifications to equipment and working methods to improve production.
- Researching technical developments within the industry and reporting to management on those of probable benefit to the company.
- Undertaking factory trials of new lines and modified technology to ensure changes introduced smoothly.

EDUCATION

MBA	Midlands University	XXXX – XXXX (part-time study)
BSc (Hons) 2:2 Mechanical Engineering	West Wales University	XXXX – XXXX
3 A-levels	Broadwick School, Crewe	XXXX – XXXX

FURTHER TRAINING

- Diploma in Quality Management awarded by Midlands College XXXX
- Certificate in Supervisory Skills awarded by Midlands College XXXX
- Training on computer programming and the Multisoft products suite

ADDITIONAL INFORMATION

- Date of birth XX/XX/XX
- Full, clean driving licence
- Excellent health
- References available on request